W9-CED-836

Getting To Know...

Nature's Children

BIGHORN SHEEP

Bill Ivy

PUBLISHER   Joseph R. DeVarennes
PUBLICATION DIRECTOR   Kenneth H. Pearson
MANAGING EDITOR   Valerie Wyatt
SERIES ADVISOR   Merebeth Switzer
SERIES CONSULTANT   Michael Singleton
CONSULTANTS   Ross James
                                      Kay McKeever
                                      Dr. Audrey N. Tomera

ADVISORS   Roger Aubin
                                      Robert Furlonger
                                      Gaston Lavoie

EDITORIAL SUPERVISOR   Jocelyn Smyth
PRODUCTION MANAGER   Ernest Homewood
PRODUCTION ASSISTANTS   Penelope Moir
                                      Brock Piper

EDITORS   Katherine Farris   Anne Minguet-Patocka
                  Sandra Gulland   Sarah Reid
                  Cristel Kleitsch   Cathy Ripley
                  Elizabeth MacLeod   Eleanor Tourtel
                  Pamela Martin   Karin Velcheff

PHOTO EDITORS   Bill Ivy
                                      Don Markle

DESIGN   Annette Tatchell
CARTOGRAPHER   Jane Davie
PUBLICATION ADMINISTRATION   Kathy Kishimoto
                                      Monique Lemonnier

ARTISTS   Marianne Collins   Greg Ruhl
                  Pat Ivy   Mary Theberge

This series is approved and recommended by the Federation of Ontario Naturalists.

Canadian Cataloguing in Publication Data

Ivy, Bill, 1953-
  Bighorn sheep

(Getting to know—nature's children)
Includes index.
ISBN 0-7172-1907-0

1. Bighorn sheep—Juvenile literature.
I. Title. II. Series.

QL737.U53I95 1985   j599.73'58   C85-098703-2

Copyright © 1985 by Grolier Limited. All rights reserved.
Printed and Bound in U.S.A.

Have you ever wondered . . .

Can you imagine what it would be like to climb one of the Rocky Mountains? You would need ropes and picks and special shoes, and it would take you many, many days.

Mountain climbing is hard work for people—but not for Bighorn Sheep. The Bighorn is a natural athlete and can move with ease through mountainous areas that would quickly tire most two-legged athletes. No wonder the Bighorn is sometimes called "King of the Mountain."

You may think that all sheep are much the same, that they are all timid and meek and that they lead rather boring and unadventurous lives. If you do, you have several surprises in store for you as you learn more about the Bighorn.

Fun and Games

Young Bighorns like playing almost as much as you do—and they even play some of the same games!

One of their favorites is follow the leader. The lambs race nimbly after each other, without even seeming to notice that they are playing on the side of a mountain!

Another favorite game is king of the castle. One lamb climbs to the top of a rockpile and dares the rest to knock it off. Whichever lamb does so becomes the new king. This game is a lot of fun, but it is also good practice for the lambs. It teaches them rock-climbing, which is an important skill for a Bighorn Sheep.

"I'm the king of the castle!"

Bighorn Country

Bighorn Sheep are found in the western mountain regions of North America. Although their range extends south to Mexico, most make their home in the Rocky Mountains of Alberta and British Columbia. Bighorns prefer to live in wilderness areas, well away from people. They spend their summers high up in the mountains. Then, when the winter snows begin, they move down into the valleys.

Where Bighorn Sheep live in North America.

Sheep Cousins

The Bighorn is closely related to farm sheep, and it also has several wild sheep cousins. Some of these live in Asia and northern Russia while others are found right here in North America. The Bighorn's closest wild cousin is the Dall's Sheep which lives in the Yukon and Alaska.

Dall's Sheep are white or gray and are found farther north than the Bighorn.

The Bighorn Up Close

At first glance it is hard to believe that the Bighorn is really a sheep at all. Its beautiful brown and white coat does not even look like wool! But the wool is there, hidden under a covering of long guard hairs. The wool traps body-warmed air close to the Bighorn's skin, while the guard hairs shed water and snow. The Bighorn's lower belly, rump and muzzle tip are all creamy white. Its short tail is dark.

A full-grown male, or ram, may stand one metre (3.3 feet) tall at the shoulder and weigh as much as 155 kilograms (340 pounds). That is almost one and a half times as big as farm sheep! The females, or ewes, are much smaller.

Notice how small and slender the ewe's horns are compared to the ram's.

Super Senses

Both rams and ewes have excellent eyesight. Their large, amber-yellow eyes can spot something eight kilometres (5 miles) away. If you wanted to see that far, you would have to look through a pair of binoculars! When you consider that the Bighorn's sense of smell and hearing are almost as sharp as its eyesight, you can understand why it is nearly impossible to sneak up on one.

A Bighorn's sharp eyesight is its best defense against approaching enemies.

Watch Out!

For part of the year, when they are high up in the mountains, full-grown Bighorns have few enemies. Only the cougar hunts there. However, the lambs must be protected from Golden Eagles. These birds are large enough to swoop down from the sky and snatch a lamb away. If a lamb senses danger, it scurries under its mother's belly, and she fends off the eagle with her horns.

During the winter on the other hand, when they are down in the mountain valleys, even full-grown Bighorns must be cautious. They must watch out for wolves, bears, coyotes, bobcats and lynx.

But catching a Bighorn is not easy! Its keen senses give it plenty of warning, and few predators are surefooted enough to chase it along the narrow mountain trails. If a Bighorn cannot outrun its enemy, it may turn and charge. Most predators would rather flee than fight a charging Bighorn.

Opposite page:

The safest place for these lambs is by their mother's side.

Grass-Loving Grazers

Bighorns, like people, have three main mealtimes each day—morning, mid-day and late afternoon. The Bighorn begins breakfast as soon as the first rays of light appear. The menu is simple and almost always the same: grass, grass and more grass! Bluegrass, Junegrass, needlegrass and wheatgrass are some of its favorites. For variety, it will eat some other plants and shrubs such as wild rose, lupines, vetch, chokeberry, horsetail and willow.

In the winter when food is scarce, the Bighorn eats less nutritious twigs, buds and even some evergreens, such as Douglas Fir. It also digs beneath the snow with its feet to get at whatever grass it can find.

Neck-deep in grass—what more could any Bighorn ask?

Eat Now, Chew Later

The Bighorn does not take a bit of food and chew it thoroughly before swallowing the way you do. Instead it swallows grass almost whole as it grazes. This unchewed food goes into a special storage stomach. Later, when the Bighorn is relaxing, it brings this food back up into its mouth and chews it. This is known as chewing its cud. You may have seen cows do the same thing.

After the cud has been chewed and swallowed again the rest of the stomach finishes digesting it. Talk about stretching out a meal!

Grasses and sedges make up 60 percent of the Bighorn's diet.

Bighorn hoof print

Opposite page:

To climb steep cliffs like these you really have to be "on your toes."

Nimble Feet

The Bighorn is as agile on its feet as any circus performer. It runs fearlessly up and down steep mountain slopes and can balance on the narrowest of ledges. If we were to try to walk on the same ice and slippery rocks as the Bighorn does, we would be sliding down the mountain on the seat of our pants in no time.

How does the Bighorn do it? The secret is in the design of its feet. The outer edge of each hoof is hard and sharp for cutting into earth, gravel and ice. The center is filled with a spongy material that provides traction. In addition the Bighorn's split hoofs pinch and hold onto the rocks a bit like clothes pegs. Two smaller claws higher up the foot serve as brakes if the Bighorn starts to slide.

The Bighorn is famous for its jumping ability. It can leap two metres (7 feet) into the air! That ability comes in handy when it must jump across a wide crevice. And if a ridge should start to break under its weight, the Bighorn can turn in mid-air and land on its feet, just like a cat!

Bighorns' Big Horns

It is certainly no mystery how the Bighorn got its name! Few animals can boast of such impressive horns. The male's horns curl like corkscrews and often form a complete circle on each side of his head. This massive headset may weigh up to 14 kilograms (30 pounds) and measure 115 centimetres (45 inches) around the curve.

Although they are very handsome, these big horns can cause problems. Not only are they heavy to carry around, but it is sometimes also difficult for the Bighorn to see around them. Rams often rub their horns against rocks to wear them down.

Often, among horned animals, only the male has horns. But this is not the case in the Bighorn family. The females, or ewes, also have horns, although they are much smaller than the rams'. Instead of curving around in circles, they curl only slightly.

A Bighorn never sheds its horns and they grow larger every year.

Opposite page:

Big Horns!

Snorts and Baas

If you could listen in on some Bighorns "talking," you might think you were in a barnyard. They sound just like their cousins, the farm sheep.

A low-pitched baa is a mother's way of calling a lamb to her. It means danger may be nearby. Lambs bleat to let their mothers know they are hungry or tired. But male Bighorns seldom talk. Instead they snort, usually to let other males know they are ready for a fight.

Like most young animals, Bighorn lambs are curious about everything and eager to explore their surroundings.

Leader of the Pack

Bighorns live in bands of anywhere from 10 to 100 sheep. During the summer, the males form their own "bachelor clubs" of about 10 rams. These male bands have a leader, often the sheep with the biggest horns. This is because large horns usually mean their owner is large and healthy. So he is a natural leader. Sometimes, other rams challenge his leadership by butting at his horns, but serious fights seldom develop.

At the same time the females and young form their own herds. Away from the males, they graze leisurely on the mountain meadows. An older, experienced ewe takes charge of the flock and stands guard as the other sheep feed. At the first sign of danger, she gives the alarm by stamping her foot. Then, she bolts away leading the fleeing band to safety high up the mountainside.

Come winter, the rams, ewes and young join together forming larger bands. They do not separate into smaller groups again until the following spring.

Opposite page:

Bighorn bachelor club.

Down from the High Country

Winters are harsh in the mountains. The Bighorn begins to prepare for bad weather by eating as much as it can to store up a thick layer of fat.

After the first heavy snowfall, the band begins its journey from the high country to the more sheltered valleys below. The same routes are used year after year. Bighorns may travel 40 kilometres (25 miles) or more before finally reaching their destination.

They travel in single file, following their leader. If anyone tries to pass the lead ram he will use his horns to keep them in line. Even though a single Bighorn can run as fast as 56 kilometres (35 miles) per hour, the band seldom travels faster than a trot. The Bighorns are good swimmers and often cross rivers and lakes along the way. From time to time the band rests. The Bighorns fold their legs under their bodies to keep warm and sleep.

Weathering the storm.

Hard Times

For a winter home, the band chooses a south-facing slope that is kept fairly clear of snow by the sun and wind. Finding enough to eat in winter is often a problem. Should the snow become too deep to paw through, many may go hungry. During a bad storm they often huddle together against a cliff or take shelter in a cave. Like many of us, the Bighorns eagerly await the arrival of spring.

Heavy snowfalls may make it difficult for Bighorns to get the food they need.

The Challenge

During November and December, once the
Bighorns are down in the valleys, a great deal
of fighting takes place among the rams of the
herd. It is mating season, and if two males
choose the same female, they will fight to see
who wins her. Their main weapon is their
mighty horns.

First the two challengers size each other up.
They lower their heads to show off their
enormous horns. Then, snorting and grunting,
they begin to push and shove each other.
Sometimes one may even kick. If one of them
does not back down they prepare for a real
"head to head" battle.

*"Getting pushy" usually starts a
battle.*

Head to Head

The Bighorns circle each other at a distance of about nine metres (10 yards). As if at a signal, they rear up on their hind legs. Then they charge, heads down, at full speed. The impact of head crashing into head sends ripples through their bodies, and the echoing crack can be heard far away.

Slightly stunned by the blow, the groggy fighters shake their heads. When the dizziness clears, they back off for another charge. Again and again they butt each other until one of them has had enough. This may take hours. Occasionally one ram may even be knocked out cold! Incredibly, very few Bighorns are ever seriously hurt. Their skulls and massive neck muscles absorb most of the force of the blows. Still, you can imagine the headaches they must get!

Head-butting duels can break out at any time of the year as Bighorns often test each other's might.

New Coats

One nice thing about spring is that you no longer have to wear your heavy winter clothes. Neither do Bighorns. Once the warmer weather reaches the mountains the Bighorns shed their thick winter coats. Their coats lighten in color and gradually thin out. At this stage they look rather shaggy with long, matted strands of their old coats hanging from their bodies. To help loosen the hair, the Bighorns rub themselves against rocks and trees.

The Bighorn's lightweight spring coat will start to thicken again in the fall—just in time for winter.

Mountain Nursery

While the Bighorns are still in the valleys, the lambs are born. The mother Bighorn leaves the herd in search of a sheltered nursery, probably a steep rock cliff or a high ledge. Usually only one lamb is born to a mother, but sometimes there are twins.

As soon as she has given birth, the ewe licks her baby's wet, woolly, light brown coat until it is dry. Then mother and baby gently touch noses to learn each other's scent.

The trembling youngster struggles to its feet and balances on wobbly legs. Only 40 centimetres (16 inches) tall, the newborn already has tiny buttons on its head where its horns will be.

As soon as it is standing the lamb cuddles under its mother's belly and begins to nurse on her milk. The proud mother baas softly to her baby, who is growing stronger every minute.

A Bighorn mother will only tend to the needs of her own young; others are ignored.

The Long Climb

The newborn lambs receive a friendly welcome
when they join the rest of the flock. Many
year-old Bighorns and single females crowd
around the newest member of the group.
Sometimes the mother and her baby sneak
away from the flock to nurse in peace!

Most human babies are about a year old
before they take their first steps on their own.
But Bighorn babies can walk when they are
only a few hours old and run and jump within
a few days.

Growing up quickly is important for a
Bighorn lamb. When it is only a few weeks old
it must join the rest of the flock as it travels
up the mountain to its summer meadows.

This is a long hard climb for the lamb. It
stays close to its mother for protection and
food.

*Even the most frolicsome youngster
needs a rest now and again.*

45

Part of the Flock

Summer is a good time for a Bighorn lamb. There is plenty of food in the mountain meadow, and bit by bit it stops nursing and starts eating grass like its mother. All that food makes the lamb strong and frisky. It is soon racing around and playing games with the other Bighorns its age. While the youngsters are having their fun, the mothers often take turns babysitting.

By the end of their first summer, the lambs weigh about 34 kilograms (75 pounds). And by the time the Bighorns are ready for their journey down the mountain to their winter home, the lambs no longer need to stay close to their mothers. They are part of the flock now, and will soon begin to raise families of their own.

Special Words

Band   A group of Bighorn Sheep.

Crevice   A gap in rock or ice.

Cud   Hastily swallowed food bought back for chewing by cud chewers such as deer, sheep and cows.

Ewe   A female Bighorn.

Guard hairs   Long coarse hairs that make up the outer layer of the Bighorn's coat.

Hoofs   Feet of sheep, deer and some other animals.

Horn   Outgrowth on head of cattle, sheep and some other animals. Unlike antlers, horns do not fall off every year.

Lamb   A young Bighorn.

Mating season   The time of year during which animals come together to produce young.

Nurse   To drink the mother's milk.

Ram   A male Bighorn.

INDEX

Cover Photo: Wayne Lankinen (Valan Photos)

Photo Credits: Stephen J. Krasemann (Valan Photos), page 4; Wayne Lankinen (Valan Photos), page 7; Brian Milne (First Light Associated Photographers), pages 8, 11, 12, 19, 35, 39, 43, 44; Thomas Kitchin (Valan Photos), pages 15, 20; J.D. Markou (Valan Photos), page 16; Esther Schmidt (Valan Photos), pages 23, 32; Hälle Flygare (Valan Photos), page 24; Tim Fitzharris (First Light Associated Photographers), pages 26, 40; K. Sommerer (Miller Services), page 28; Dennis Schmidt (Valan Photos), page 31; T. Ulrich (Miller Services), pages 36-37.

Getting To Know...

Nature's Children

PRAIRIE DOGS

Celia B. Lottridge
and
Susan Horner

PUBLISHER	Joseph R. DeVarennes
PUBLICATION DIRECTOR	Kenneth H. Pearson
MANAGING EDITOR	Valerie Wyatt
SERIES ADVISOR	Merebeth Switzer
SERIES CONSULTANT	Michael Singleton
CONSULTANTS	Ross James
	Kay McKeever
	Dr. Audrey N. Tomera
ADVISORS	Roger Aubin
	Robert Furlonger
	Gaston Lavoie
EDITORIAL SUPERVISOR	Jocelyn Smyth
PRODUCTION MANAGER	Ernest Homewood
PRODUCTION ASSISTANTS	Penelope Moir
	Brock Piper

EDITORS

Katherine Farris   Anne Minguet-Patocka
Sandra Gulland   Sarah Reid
Cristel Kleitsch   Cathy Ripley
Elizabeth MacLeod   Eleanor Tourtel
Pamela Martin   Karin Velcheff

PHOTO EDITORS	Bill Ivy
	Don Markle
DESIGN	Annette Tatchell
CARTOGRAPHER	Jane Davie
PUBLICATION ADMINISTRATION	Kathy Kishimoto
	Monique Lemonnier

ARTISTS

Marianne Collins   Greg Ruhl
Pat Ivy   Mary Theberge

This series is approved and recommended by the Federation of Ontario Naturalists.

Canadian Cataloguing in Publication Data

Lottridge, Celia.
   Prairie dogs

(Getting to know—nature's children)
Includes index.
ISBN 0-7172-1939-9

1. Prairie dogs—Juvenile literature.
I. Horner, Susan.   II. Title.   III. Series.

QL737.R68L68 1985   j599.32'32   C85-098730-X

Copyright © 1985 by Grolier Limited. All rights reserved.
Printed and Bound in U.S.A.

Have you ever wondered . . .

Prairie Dogs

Some wild animals live alone, some live with a mate and some live in family groups. But there is one kind of wild animal that lives with hundreds of others in a town. This animal is the Prairie Dog.

Imagine that you are visiting a Prairie Dog town very early on a summer morning. The first thing you would see is a flat, grassy prairie dotted with low mounds of dirt. A closer look at one of these mounds would reveal a hole. This is the entrance to a Prairie Dog's home.

If you watched this entrance carefully you might see a small tan head poke up out of it. But one move from you and the Prairie Dog would disappear back down the hole. It might pop up again though, if you waited very quietly, and maybe even come out for a look around.

Rise and Shine

When the Prairie Dog comes out of its den, you can see that it is about the size of a plump puppy. Not including its tail, it is about 36 centimetres (14 inches) long and covered with thick tan and brown fur that is almost the same color as the dried earth around its home. Its body is plump, and its short tail—10 centimetres (4 inches) long—sticks out behind.

If the Prairie Dog sees nothing to disturb it, it tilts back its head and makes a few short, sharp sounds, or chirks. With each chirk its tail quivers and seems to signal "all clear!"

Soon more Prairie Dogs come out of their homes. They greet each other by kissing and nuzzling. When morning greetings are over, the business of the day begins. The Prairie Dogs feed busily, bask in the sun, take dust baths, visit neighbors or wash themselves.

A new day is underway in the Prairie Dog town.

"All clear!"

Are Prairie Dogs Really Dogs?

There are five kinds of Prairie Dogs in North America. The most common are the Black-tailed and White-tailed Prairie Dogs. Except for the color of their tails, they look very much alike.

The Black-tailed Prairie Dog is found on flat prairies from southern Saskatchewan to Oklahoma and Texas. The White-tailed Prairie Dog lives farther west, in the treeless foothills of Colorado, Utah and New Mexico.

Because their alarm call sounds like the bark of a small dog, early prairie settlers called them Prairie Dogs or prairie barkers. But Prairie Dogs are not really dogs. They are rodents and are related to the mouse, chipmunk, beaver and, most closely, to the Ground Squirrel. Like all rodents they are gnawers. Their teeth are especially good for biting through tough roots and stalks.

From the front it is hard to know which kind of Prairie Dog you are looking at. But the tail will tell you who is who.

Prairie Dog Homes

The hole at the top of a Prairie Dog mound is the entrance to the Prairie Dog's burrow home. The entrance hall is a long tunnel three to four metres (10 to 14 feet) straight down. Then it levels off, continuing deep underground for about the length of a city backyard. Halfway down the entrance tunnel is a shelf where the Prairie Dog can turn around or hide in case of danger.

Small side tunnels lead to sleeping rooms, bathrooms and a larger room where the babies are born. The main tunnel often continues past the bedrooms, joining several burrows together. This way, neighbors can visit without going outside!

The burrow is warm in winter and cool in summer because it is so deep. And it stays dry because the entrance tunnel goes down steeply and then turns up again. Water cannot flow into the tunnels beyond.

Cut-away of a Prairie Dog burrow.

Miniature Mountains

As Prairie Dogs dig their burrows, they push the loose earth out of the tunnel with their foreheads, until there is a pile of dirt at the entrance. They scrape up more earth from around the edges of the pile to make it bigger. Then they butt at the loose heap of dirt with their foreheads and noses until they have shaped it into a firm mound. If you looked carefully at a mound you might see the owner's nose prints.

Prairie Dogs spend a lot of time on their mounds sunning themselves and chatting to each other. Young Prairie Dogs play by climbing up and down these miniature mountains.

These mounds are very important to Prairie Dogs. Because they are higher than the flat land around them they make good lookout posts. By standing on its mound and stretching as tall as possible, a Prairie Dog has a good view all around. The mound also makes a dam to keep any runoff from rain showers from flowing into the burrow entrance.

Opposite page:

This Prairie Dog is hard at work building up its mound.

A Close-knit Community

Prairie Dogs live in groups called coteries. A coterie may start with only one male and one female, but it soon grows to include other adults, some young ones called yearlings and a number of babies. Some coteries have as many as 35 members, but most have fewer than a dozen.

A coterie builds as many burrows and mounds as are needed to hold all of its members. Digging the burrows and keeping them in good repair is a big job, and all the Prairie Dogs in the coterie help with the work. They use their long front claws and short strong legs for digging and their sharp teeth for cutting through roots.

Home on the Range.

Top Dog

The mounds and burrows where a coterie lives and some of the land around them are the territory of that coterie. Visitors are not welcome.

Each coterie is headed by the strongest male. He is the one who comes out of the hole first in the morning and goes in last at night. He knows exactly how much territory belongs to his coterie. If he finds a member of another coterie in his territory he gets to work. He scolds the intruder noisily to scare it off and sometimes even gives the stranger a quick bite on the rump. OUCH!

■ *Black-tailed Prairie Dog*
■ *White-tailed Prairie Dog*

Prairie Dog Town

The territories of many coteries taken together form a Prairie Dog town. Prairie Dog towns, like those people live in, may be large or small. One huge town that existed in Texas many years ago held 400 million Prairie Dogs. It should have been called Prairie Dog City!

Most Prairie Dog towns are much smaller than that, however. Usually they cover about 80 hectares (200 acres) and are home to about 140 coteries or over 1000 Prairie Dogs.

And, like towns people live in, Prairie Dog towns are divided into smaller units, a bit like our blocks. These are called wards and are separated from each other by things such as hills, trees and different kinds of grass.

Prairie Dog village.

Keeping Watch

Every adult Prairie Dog spends some time being a sentinel. While the other Prairie Dogs sun themselves, eat or play, the sentinel sits on its haunches on top of the mound and looks for signs of danger.

If a sentinel sees the shadow of a hawk, hears the yip of a coyote or senses any unusual movement nearby, it sounds the alarm. To do this it rises up on its toes, flicks its tail and barks loudly. Quick as a flash, all the Prairie Dogs dive into their burrows for safety.

For a few moments, all is quiet. Then the sentinel pokes up its head. If the danger has passed, an "all clear" chirk sounds. As quickly as they had disappeared, all the Prairie Dogs pop out of their burrows to resume their busy lives.

At the first sign of danger this alert Prairie Dog will sound the alarm.

Who Goes There?

Prairie Dogs use touch and smell to recognize the members of their coterie. They know each other very well because they spend a lot of time stroking or grooming each other with their paws. They often groom each other while they sun themselves. They also rub necks and kiss frequently while they are building mounds or looking for food.

Because they know the touch and smell of each other so well they can easily tell friend from stranger. That is why Prairie Dogs greet each other with a kiss. That kiss lets each dog get a good sniff of the other.

Mother and pup greet each other with a kiss.

What's for Dinner?

Prairie Dogs do not have to travel far to find food. They eat the grasses and other leafy plants that grow around their mounds. They choose their favorites by smell and nip the plants off neatly with their sharp teeth. Then they sit up, hold the stem or leaf in their front paws and nibble away. The Prairie Dogs' grassy diet has a useful side effect: all the munching keeps the grass around their mounds well trimmed and gives them a good view over their territory.

Plants also provide Prairie Dogs with the water they need. The stalks of prickly thistles are especially juicy. Prairie Dogs are careful to bite the stalks close to the ground so that they will not get pricked.

In the summer, Prairie Dogs spend more than half of their waking hours eating. It is important for them to eat and get fat while plants are green and plentiful, for in winter food is hard to find.

Opposite page:

Like their relatives the squirrels, Prairie Dogs hold food in their front paws.

Sun Worshippers

Prairie Dogs love warm sunny days. They spend their time waddling about their territory, eating, repairing their mounds, greeting each other with kisses, grooming each other and keeping watch.

If it gets too hot in the middle of the day, they will go into their burrows for a while. Rain, too, will drive them inside. After a rain, though, they love to come out and eat, for the plants are moist and delicious.

Wind makes Prairie Dogs uneasy, probably because the sound of it covers up sounds that might warn them of approaching danger. On windy days they are especially alert and will duck into their holes at any unusual movement.

Fattening up for winter!

A Cozy Retreat

As winter approaches Prairie Dogs concentrate on getting fat. In cold weather, they slow down and spend most of their time in their burrows. But they do not go into a deep sleep and hibernate, as some squirrels do. When the winter weather is fine, Prairie Dogs pop out for a look around and a quick snack on whatever food they can find. However, when winter winds blow, they retreat to the warmth of their underground home.

Prairie Dogs line their bedrooms with dried grasses and weeds.

Mating Time

In early spring, Prairie Dogs become lively again. Food is still hard to find, but they come out of their holes to feel the warmth of the sunshine and greet each other. Soon all the coteries in the town are out. The mounds are abuzz with activity and with the chirking, yipping conversation of Prairie Dogs.

Mating time is March and April. Then, both males and females clean out the old burrows and dig new tunnels. The adult females line the largest sleeping room in the burrow with soft, dry grass to make nests for the babies that will soon be born.

Although young Prairie Dogs are very curious they must be sure to stay close to home.

Prairie Dog Pups

The babies are born in late May. There are usually four or five babies in a litter. They are red, wrinkled, hairless, blind little things about eight centimetres (3 inches) long from nose to tail.

The mother looks after her babies carefully. For the first few weeks she allows no one else near them. She begins to get them ready for a life of grooming and kissing by licking and rubbing them frequently.

The pups grow fast on their mother's rich milk. In three weeks their fur has grown in. Now they can squeak and roll around a little.

At about five weeks they open their eyes. They are starting to look a lot like their parents. Soon they are running around the burrow, trying to bark. And it is not long until the great day when they come out of their holes and tumble down their mounds into the great wide world.

"Pass it on!"

Bringing Up the Babies

Once the pups have come out of their burrows, everyone in the Prairie Dog town helps raise and care for them. The little ones run from one burrow to another to play with the babies from other litters. Sometimes they sleep over at another pup's home. Unlike adult Prairie Dogs, they are even allowed to visit other coteries.

Both male and female adults spend much time grooming the pups, kissing them and playing chasing and tumbling games with them. The pups love these games so much that they sometimes become nuisances. An adult who is trying to keep watch or eat has to discourage them with little nips or pushes.

The babies soon learn to dart into their holes if anything strange happens. They pop in and out of their holes hundreds of times a day like furry little jack-in-the-boxes.

But their babyhood is short. At seven weeks of age, they can find and eat food on their own. At 10 weeks, they are able to look after themselves.

Opposite page:

The tan and brown coat of the Prairie Dog blends in with the soil of the mound.

Learning to be Prairie Dogs

Toward summer's end, the spring babies are nearly as big as their parents. Their playing has taught them how to recognize each other, how to groom and "talk" to each other.

Now they begin to learn about territories. They are no longer welcome in the territory of other coteries. They will be driven back to their own territory if they venture far.

They love to copy the older Prairie Dogs. By copying, they learn how to find food, how to respond to alarm calls and how to give calls themselves.

One call the young Prairie Dogs especially like is the territorial call, which seems to mean "Here I am and here is my territory." To give it, the Prairie Dog stands on its hind legs, thrusts its front paws out, raises its nose to the sky and gives a loud two-note bark. The young ones practice this endlessly. Sometimes they get so excited that they lean too far back and tumble over and over, down the mound.

Growing Families

By late summer, the young Prairie
Dogs, like the older ones, spend
most of their time eating to store
fat for the winter. They will spend
the winter in the burrow where
they were born. In the spring they
will be yearlings. Then they will
welcome the new litters of babies
in the coterie. By the time they are
two years old, they will be ready
to mate and have babies.

Moving On

A coterie cannot keep growing forever or there will not be enough food for all of its members. So every year some Prairie Dogs have to leave their coteries.

Yearling males sometimes go off to establish coteries of their own. Sometimes an adult male and female may go together and build new burrows and new mounds, leaving the younger members of their original coterie to carry on. Females sometimes leave to join other coteries.

New coteries, new mounds and new burrows will all become part of the Prairie Dog town where Prairie Dogs stand sentinel, work and play together.

Prairie Dogs will only travel as far from their den as they have to when looking for food.

Special Words

Burrow   A hole in the ground dug by an animal to be used as a home.

Coterie   A group of Prairie Dogs made up of 8 to 35 members.

Litter   Group of animal brothers and sisters born together.

Mating season   The time of year when animals come together to produce young.

Prairie   A flat treeless area where grasses grow.

Pup   Young Prairie Dog.

Rodent   An animal with a certain kind of teeth, which are especially good for gnawing.

Sentinel   A guard that watches for danger and signals alarm if necessary.

Territory   Area that an animal or group of animals lives in and often defends from other animals of the same kind.

Ward   Sub-division of a Prairie Dog town.

Yearling   Animal that is once year old.

INDEX

Cover Photo: Barry Ranford

Photo Credits: Dennis Schmidt (Valan Photos), pages 4, 26; Brian Milne (First Light Associated Photographers), pages 7, 12; Stephen J. Krasemann (Valan Photos), pages 8, 25, 33, 34, 37, 43; Esther Schmidt (Valan Photos), pages 15, 21, 40; Robert C. Simpson (Valan Photos), page 16; Wayne Lankinen (Valan Photos), pages 18-19, 29, 30, 46; Wilf Schurig (Valan Photos), page 22; Thomas Kitchin (Valan Photos), page 44.